Tiny Dinosaurs

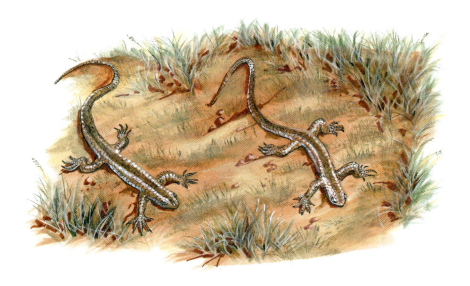

Story by Heather Hammonds

Illustrations by Jenny Mountstephen

"It's our school Open House in two weeks time," said Mrs. Young. "The principal would like each class to put on a display in the school hall. You have done some excellent work in science this year, and I would like you all to choose something you were really interested in during the year for your project."

"Let's do a project together," said Amy, to her twin sister Grace.

"I liked learning about wild animals," said Grace.

"But we can't put wild animals in our display," said Amy.

"Yes we can," said Grace. "I've seen wild animals here on the school grounds."

"You have not!" giggled Amy.

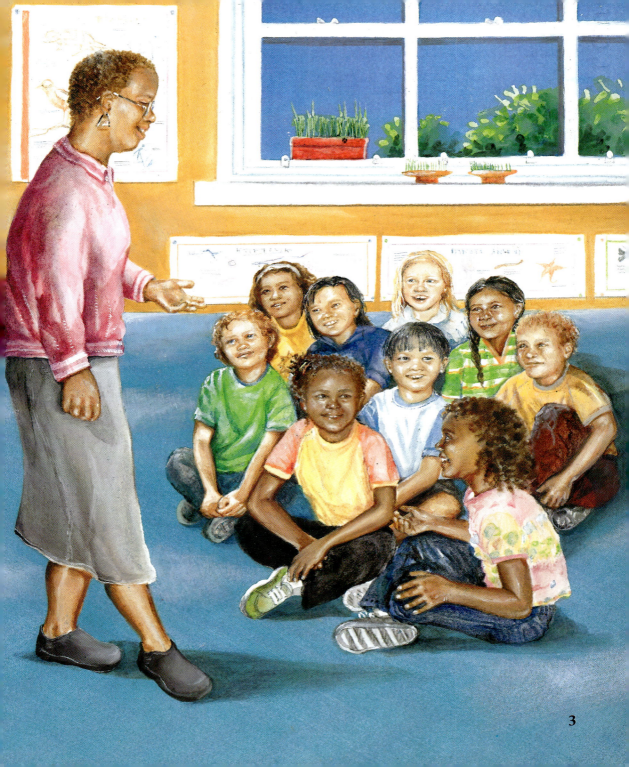

3

"What about all those lizards in the grass by the back fence?" said Grace. "They're wild animals."

In the sunny weather, lots of small lizards darted around in the grass, flicking their tongues and eating insects.

"How could we use lizards in our project?" asked Amy.

"We could put soil and rocks and other things inside our old fish tank," said Grace. "We could make it look like a prehistoric world, and if we catch some of those lizards and put them in the tank, they might look like tiny dinosaurs."

5

When they arrived home, the girls found the fish tank and cleaned it out with soapy water. Then they spread soil on the bottom of the tank. They made a volcano out of modeling clay and put it in one corner. Amy poured some mud into the crater until it overflowed. It looked as though lava was running down the sides of the volcano.

"I think we need a lake," said Amy, so she put a plastic bowl full of water in the middle of the tank. Grace found some twigs that were just like little trees, and placed them around the bowl. When the twins had finished, the fish tank looked like a little prehistoric world.

"All we need now are the lizards," said Amy. "We'll catch them tomorrow."

At lunchtime the next day, the girls hurried outside to find some lizards.

"There's one!" whispered Grace. She quickly grabbed it and put it inside Amy's lunch box. Amy saw another lizard, and they managed to catch that one, too. They carried the lunch box carefully into the classroom and put it underneath their desk.

The teacher began to read to the class, and everyone was quiet, enjoying the story. Grace noticed that the lid was starting to come off Amy's lunch box, so she reached down and pushed it back on.

"What have you got there?" frowned Mrs. Young, as she put her book down.

"Two lizards," said Grace. "Amy and I caught them at lunchtime, for our project."

"We've made a prehistoric world inside a fish tank," explained Amy, "and we're going to put the lizards into it."

Mrs. Young smiled at the girls and said, "You've thought of a good idea for your project, but lizards can die if they are taken away from their natural environment. They must be very frightened, trapped inside your lunch box."

Amy was disappointed. "I guess we'll have to let them go," she said.

Mrs. Young took the class outside, and everyone watched as Amy and Grace crouched down and opened the lunch box. As soon as the lizards were free, they darted off into the grass.

"I think Mrs. Young was right," whispered Grace. "Those poor lizards must have been very scared when we caught them."

"But our prehistoric world won't look any good without them," sighed Amy.

Later that afternoon, the girls sat in their room staring at the fish tank.

"I can't think of anything else to put in our prehistoric world," said Grace miserably. "It would have looked fantastic with the lizards as tiny dinosaurs. Now we'll have to start another project."

"I've got an idea!" shouted Amy, jumping up with excitement. She ran over to the closet. After hunting around at the back of a shelf, she pulled out a bag of plastic dinosaurs. "These will be much better than live lizards," she said. "They will make it look even more like a prehistoric world."

"You're right," said Grace. "Let's make some cards to go beside our display."

"Yes," said Amy. "I'll get the dinosaur books."

On the night of the Open House, Mom and Dad helped the girls carry their project into the school hall. Many children and their parents were already there looking at the displays.

Grace and Amy put their prehistoric world on a table beside other projects from their class.

After everyone had arrived and the children had set up their displays, the principal walked slowly around the room admiring the projects. He stopped to talk to Grace and Amy.

"A prehistoric world complete with tiny dinosaurs and lava coming out of a volcano," he said. Then he picked up a card and began to read it aloud. Everyone turned to listen to him. "This information is very interesting," the principal said. "You've put a lot of work into your project."

Prehistoric
World

wheat

where
does bread
come
from?

15

"Well done, girls," smiled Mrs. Young. "It was a much better idea to use plastic dinosaurs instead of those poor little lizards."

"We think so too," said Amy.

"These dinosaurs aren't scared at all," laughed Grace.